THE BLOCK TO THE BOARDROOM

Discover how four spiritual women
live, love, & grow in a post-9/11
era. Based on true events.
Inspired by and an homage to Real
Hip-Hop and MCs

First edition published: March 6, 2020

I0052650

The Block to the
Boardroom

بسم الله الرحمٰن الرحيم

Dedicated to my parents.

الله blessed me tremendously by choosing you

as my Mom & Dad!

ال حمد لله

جزاك الله خير for your unconditional love,

support, fierce protection, & the innumerable sacrifices including, but not limited to, comfort, wealth, & unfortunately dignity to give your kids, & especially daughters, a better life

.ال حمد لله وما شاء الله

Impossible to repay you. Pray I am a coolness

to your eyes, صدقة الجارية

and make you proud.

Love you to جنّةُ فردوس!♥ ♥ ♥

Welcome to the world of Noura, Khadijah, Sara, & Isabella. Follow the professional & dating lives of these four dynamic women as they navigate the world of Corporate America, matchmaking aunties, mansplaining, all the "isms", & the cultural & family traditions that are as unique as they are.

Noura, single Desi Muslim CTO, is BFF with Khadijah, an African-American Senior HR married to her high school sweetheart. Adding to this dynamic duo are Sara, a Palestinian artist in a long-term relationship & Isabella, Christian Latina that hasn't landed on a career or partner.

As Chief Technology Officer of a Fortune 100 company, Noura should get the respect & authority that the title elicits. But it's not given to her because her industry is filled with microaggression, mansplaining, & shade from the predominantly white, old Republican men that control it. John, her most aggressive & jealous colleague, takes every opportunity to undermine & challenge her. Noura is taken aback when a long-standing client insinuates that she may have ties to a terrorist organization. John seizes on the client's fear to fan the flames of hatred & bigotry against Noura.

Noura is in an on again/off again with her childhood sweetheart Hakim. When they're off again, she dates any & every available Muslim man in the hopes of finding her future husband. She & Hakim were intended to get married but then

Hakim completely changed. He became violent at times & angry. Some days he would abruptly end the relationship & others he couldn't live without her. Noura still loves Hakim but doesn't know how to help him. She's dating Dawud when Hakim isn't in the picture.

Dawud is nice & they work well on paper. But he doesn't excite her passion like Hakim. Having never been married, Noura doesn't know what makes a marriage work & whether she should continue to search for passion or settle for boring stability. Through her life experiences, Noura learns, grows, & evolves.

Khadijah, Sara, & Isabella are Noura's closest friends, advisors, & party crew. Khadijah is an African-American mental health counselor married to her high school sweetheart for 18 years. They are marriage & relationship goals. Though she was born & raised Muslim, other Muslims assume she converted from the Nation of Islam. This irritates Khadijah & exacerbates the divide between desi & African-American Muslims. Khadijah is a champion of mental health for others but doesn't use her own training to handle her own emotions. She works in melanated communities & sees the detrimental impact from lack of education, support, & wealth. She became a mother so young that she is unclear of her identity outside of her roles as wife & mother of three. She fights tirelessly to advocate to reduce the stigma of mental health while being an amazing wife & mother.

Sara's parents are refugees from Palestine. Her Baba is the only survivor in his family & the guilt & shame of that is so pronounced that it's a fourth family member. Baba constantly reminds Sara how happy it makes him that she reminds him of his dead sister, Jamillah. Sara adores her Baba & desperately wants him to have happiness in his life. She strives to live up to the saintly image of Jamillah. She even went as far as becoming a nurse to fulfill Jamillah's career aspirations at 7 when she was killed. But Sara despises nursing. The sight of blood always has & still makes her nauseous. At 33, & after an especially horrific night in the hospital, Sara's resolve falters. She's unsure how much longer she can maintain the charade for her Baba.

Isabella converted from Catholicism. Though they have different beliefs, she & Noura connect over their mutual love for God & the 96% of their religions that are identical. Her strong faith is tested when she discovers that her husband of 5 years, Frank, cheated. She feels betrayed not only by Frank but by the Christian community. Their mutual friends either turned a blind eye or take Frank's side & blame Isabella for "pushing him to cheat". She feels isolated in her faith community, pendulums between forgiving Frank (based on her faith) or cursing him out, setting his things on fire, & divorcing him (not so faith based).

The Block to the
Boardroom

Songs (Chapters)

١.   **Opening**: **Her Story** (inspired by: Slick Rick: Children's Story)

٢.   **My Life You Stole (Amreekie)** (inspired by: Eric B: I Know You Got Soul)

٣. **Dear Mama** (inspired by: Tupac: Dear Mama)

٤.   **Start of the Fall** (inspired by: TLC: Waterfalls) /Life After Death (my 9/11 survival story)

٥.   **Trial Part One: Opening Remarks** (inspired by: Redhead Kingpin: Do the Right Thing)

٦.   **Deen & the Dollar** (inspired by: KRS One: Step into Our World)

٧.   **John Smith** (inspired by: MC Lyte: Paper Thin)

٨.   **Love Letter**

٩.   دعاء **Up** (inspired by: Tupac: Hit em up)

٠١.   **Trial Part Two: Betrayals** (inspired by: Nas: Made You Look)

١١.   **Black Love/Khadijah** (inspired by: D'Angelo: Brown Sugar)

٢١.   **Muslim Representative**

٣١.   **Sara** (inspired by: Salt N Pepa: Express Yourself)

٤١.   **Isabella** (inspired by: Roxanne: Roxanne's Revenge)

٥١.   **Appropriating April** (inspired by: Lauryn Hill: Lost Ones)

٦١.   **White privilege playing tricks on me** – Ode to Corporate America (inspired by: Mind Playing Tricks On Me)

٧١. **Lifestyles of the weak & the shameless** (inspired by: Lost Boys: Lifestyles of the Rich & the Famous)

Epilogue:

Introvert

Know الله **Loves Me**

۱. Opening: Her Story (inspired by: Slick Rick: Children's Story)

Setting: Packed courtroom in major city. Reporters are buzzing outside & overcrowded the courtroom. Jeremy (Noura's attorney), Tom Jade, is making opening arguments. All of Noura's friends are there to support her (Khadijah, Sara, & Isabella) along with character witnesses for both sides.

Jeremy (Noura's attorney):

Here's a story about a girl chasing her dream
Worked her butt off, gave it all for that CREAM
cuz cash rules everything not just around her
how this world runs, no money? no one's concerned

Bought her dream house & was so happy
Didn't know her town was so crappy
Mayor's office did nothing at all
Despite 300+ emails & all her calls

Neighbor's tree about to crash through her home
But they do nothing, investors never home
Trigger after trigger after trigger after trigger
Zero help from her political figures

They didn't care cuz she's not a white man
Begged & pleaded for help from da man

Neighbor's trash attracting vermin
Former convicted Mayor giving HER a sermon
About his power, who he used to be,
Still arrogant with multiple felonies
Roof now leaking, investor not fixing
She reports it, they say she'll get the ticket
Driveway, always blocked
Woman doesn't move so she calls the cops
They escalate & abandon her
Scared cops, there's nothing worse!

Attacker tells her I'll eff you up
go back to your country
Black on brown islamophobia, travesty
Cops treat her like she's the criminal
Screech stop recording, behavior abysmal

2 men with guns afraid of a phone
She's standing exposed, all alone
Terrified thought she'd be killed
Calls her brother, he has her Will
He says leave him alone, you're too much drama
Attacker is approaching, she thinks of her Mama

& then…she just snaps
Didn't start this fight, but she will fight back
Shoots the woman right in the forehead
On the run before she..hits the ground, dead
No one to turn to, doesn't know what to do
Tweets at CAIR, ACLU & NYU
Muslims always preaching, we're an Ummah
Love for your brothers always the Kutbah

Surely they'll help in her time of need
Her Imam does nothing, despite all his leads
Just one tweet, he could've gotten her some help
A true Imam ain't it for himself

To ACLU to plead her case
Don't have an appt, they're busy, go away
Shoots the guards for being so nasty
Mistreated for years, so a killer she'll be
Next time they'll listen to someone in need

She runs next door Shaun King's paper!
Starting North Star, surely he'll save her
He doesn't work here, go away
She's had enough so she starts to spray

On the move again, they call it in
"Terrorist on the run, tell the Mayor he'll win".
Nothing rallies people like fear & hate
Just what they wanted, they salivate

She knows where..her last target will be
Walks in & calmly proceeds
Starts at the entrance, blows away the guards
Alarms go off but she stays calm

Takes everyone out, now she's in the Mayor's office
paramour on their knees, "Disturbing your conference?"
Startled, grabs his mistress as a shield
They struggle but his strength won't yield

The Block to the
                                                    Boardroom

Shoots them both, crimson pools the blouse
Underestimated her, thought she was a mouse
Both the mother bear, defending her cub
& the inner child just trying to get some love

With the mission over, she drops to her knees
Hands up, don't shoot, surrendered peacefully
But because Black Lives really don't matter
they come in hot, her body is shattered
Unload all their guns, her body actually pops
Up from sheer force & they still don't stop
Swiss-cheesed by bullets, can't count them all
Note on her chest says society's fault

Access to guns easier than healthcare
All she wanted was for someone to care
Now retrace her steps, detailed timeline
Interview people that say she seemed fine

She was..,til you pushed her to the edge
& no one was there to walk her off the ledge
So she jumped, suicide by cop
Right before death, prayed for violence to stop

٢. My Life You Stole (Amreekie) (inspired by: Eric B: I Know You Got Soul)

Setting: Noura's family's home in India.

Noura:

It's been a long time, since I left you
Living in America, doing what I had to do
Trying to blend in, be the model minority
Show em that I'm not different, we're the same see
But all that work was for naught
Because at the end, the same I'm not
Now I'm back home with the crowds & noise
It stinks! Like a farm & sweaty boys

Everyone & their mother, came to meet me
All 11 of us, crammed in the Camry
That's right 11, they made us fit
Luggage on top, kid on the gearshift
The sight, so absurd
As if there aren't bigger cars in the world

Luggage on top, us crammed inside
"Kithna dhayr luggaing gah?" I asked, worried about the ride
An elephant
on top of an ant
But they weren't fazed, all happy to see me
My Mamu kept looking over at me
"Thoo, bilqul same hay, sif lumba hogee"
I laughed at his miming stretching me

Kind of them to be so nice to me
Will they find out I'm a terrorist?
Never thought my life would go like this

[HOOK]
My Life You Stole, You Got It
My Life You Stole, You Got It

Missing my city, my spacious condo
Counting the 3 weeks, until I can go home
News should die down hopefully by then
Couldn't believe this was really happening
"Challo" my uncle said
"Aree" & with him I went

Took the dusty roads to the town
Couldn't believe number of cows around
Roaming the streets as if that's normal
Why does India have to be so third world Intelligence
abounds in this country
But still believing cows are worth worshipping
Blows my mind that I'm from here
Feel no connection, can't stand the atmosphere

Later couldn't sleep in the hot room
Solo, everyone else in the next room
Had the one bed, all to myself
They insisted, even though I felt
Selfish, them all on the floor
But jetlag hit me, couldn't protest anymore
They have no concept of personal space
Coming so close, all up in my face
Reema kept getting closer as I backed up

You do that in NY, you get messed up
Tried to explain that but she wasn't getting it
Might as well have been talking about penguins
Though NY & Mumbai, both big cities
Their worlds apart, literally & figuratively
Though the NY subways were tight
Nothing compared to here, packed so tight
People even on top of the train
One inch away from a smashed brain
Tossed & turned, fitful sleep
Don't know how I'll last 3 weeks

Awoke to smell of fresh roti
Delicious aroma wafting in, waking me
Came out the bedroom to wash my face
Surprised how many people filled the place
Couldn't remember anyone's name
Said "Assalaam alaikum" as I made my way
To the kitchen, Mamu's source of pride
Remembering Mom listening to him describe
It, sitting patiently
In her own kitchen, dwarfs his, this times 3
Not really a kitchen, more of an alley
But better than before, undoubtedly
He was so eager to impress his big sis
Thinking of Mom, now home I miss

In the kitchen stood a girl, 10 or 11
Rolling out the dough, it smelled like heaven
As she dropped the balls of dough, clouds billowed up
Flour clouds coming up in a puff
The ghee sizzled in the large pan

As she expertly rolled it…out by hand
Into perfect circles, a unique skill
One I still didn't have to this day still
My rotis…more circle-inspired
& not quite so soft, it made me tired
When Mom tried to teach me how
At that time, hating my roots, regretting that now
Flour/water proportions never figured out
& no time, to try to learn it now
The girl flipped them deftly as they puffed
No spatula needed, by hand she threw them up

"May madath kursakthee?" I asked
She looked at me shocked & seeming embarrassed
"Nahi, nahi, may abee lakay athee." She said, her face
flushed
Almost shoved me out, not sure why the fuss

In the living room I asked my aunt,
What her name was, why my help she didn't want
Everyone burst out laughing, I didn't get the joke
"Thoo naukher bunghai?" ridiculing me as she spoke
How was I supposed to know, we don't help the help?
In America, did everything for myself
Class system here, really ridiculous
Guess I should be grateful that I'm blessed
Not to be a servant or part of the outcast
Lifetime sentences, generations they last

Day dragged by, not much to do
Later that night, trying to sleep in the hot room
Hearing all the chatter since the "door" just a curtain

Couldn't understand all of it, but making fun of me I'm certain
They laughed, about my accent, my Urdu so bad
Now my turn to be embarrassed & also mad
Not like I was ever taught formally
My Urdu didn't sound that bad to me
But they were all taking turns mocking me
Calling me ABCD & "Amreekie"

Maybe coming here was a mistake
Couldn't sleep, all night lay awake
There too Desi, here too Amreekie
Who the hell…was I supposed to be
At least we don't drive crammed like a clown car
Thought back, to what brought me this far
Away from home, escaping the judgement
Couldn't wait to get back to my apartment
Got out right before the headlines hit
All over the news, "Noura – The terrorist"
Will have to go back, return eventually
My running didn't help, made me look guilty

But needed time to figure out my next move, time to think
As the life I knew, exploded in a wink
Years of hard work, earned me no credibility
Guess only one I had fooled was me

Thought Mark or Dave would have my back
10 years of friendship, gone like that
Birthday parties & babysitting their kids
But when it came down to it, no effs did they give
Let me go as if I meant nothing

Without a second thought, didn't even see it coming
Blind & dumb I was before
But they'll all learn when I settle the score

[HOOK]
My Life You Stole, You Got It
My Life You Stole, You Got It

٣. **Dear Mama** (inspired by: Tupac: Dear Mama)

Noura:

When I was young, Mom & I didn't get along
Different from everyone, danced to my own song
You didn't understand it, wanted me to get in line
Because with 8 kids you don't have time
to give attention to each one individually
But you have no idea what that did to me
So scared of you, being so hard
Now I know, result of your own trauma scars
You did the best you could with 8 kids
Dad working 3 jobs, don't know how you did it
Taking jobs that were beneath both of you
But you did them with dignity, hey
& that example is what you gave…to me
I am in awe of how you made it work
Make it with no support
No one looking out, it breaks my heart
When I hear how you were treated at the start
Not like the King & Queen you were
Underestimated, disrespected,

Wish I could take the pain away,
But even in the dark, there were brighter days
Thought you were the one always saying no
Didn't know it was Dad who told you, made it so
You took a lot of hits being the one at home
Trying to keep all of us safe, feeling alone
You didn't have any support, was no Internet

Don't know how you did it, your love I won't forget
Were & still a lion, always protecting your cubs
There is nothing as deep & strong as your love
Still remember you coming to my school
Defending me against those fools
Who said I cheated, didn't deserve my grades
You asked me once if I did it
When I said no, you said you'd take care of it
Took on that 10 person tribunal in your shalwar kameez
They tried to play you but you wouldn't let them play me
They underestimated you because of your clothes
Didn't know, they were going against a warrior, the wrong
fight they chose
You took them all out one by one, I heard it all sitting
outside
& your strength & loyalty to me still makes me cry
You always have my back & I'm so grateful
Wish we'd had this relationship when I was so little
Because I didn't understand that you were stressed
I just didn't know why I was born into that mess
Hearing your Mom say you're useless, wish you'd not been
born
Makes you wonder why God gives a woman 8 children
when she wanted none
For years I held resentment & bitterness
Searched for love from anyone & anything that didn't make
me feel useless
I still remember the Cabbage Patch Kid you gave me
Even though you nor Dad never understood why it
appealed to me
It was so ugly & crazy expensive
But you still bought it for me, your love is endless

The Block to the
                                    Boardroom

It was sitting on my bed on my birthday
When I woke up, couldn't believe it was for me
Got one for sis too, so much money wasted
To make your kids happy, wanna bring smile to your face
You are appreciated

٤. Start of the Fall (inspired by: TLC: Waterfalls)

Setting: Generic office building. Noura is sitting in her corner office, staring out of the large plate glass window overlooking the city.

Noura:

Still fresh like it was yesterday
Even though so many days
Have come & gone the memory wont fade away
Him in the ladies room pushing up on me
Wouldn't back up, hands all over me
Took my being nice for flirting as if I wanted him
Doesn't matter that his wife just gave birth to twins
He didn't do it for me which he hated
Cuz my men need to be more melanated

Was nice to him only cause I had to be
If you don't smile they ask why you so angry
Did all I could to blend in, model minority
Worked my butt off to be what they wanted me to be
Laughed at the corny jokes, let them think we were friends
But none of that mattered in the end
When lies were spread, they believed them
No one stood up or came to my defense &
15 years of friendship gone in a blink
Of an eye, shocked no one stood by my side
But guess it should've been expected
Never really belong, never really accepted
Only keep us around to serve them, make them richer
When things go down, no one flees quicker

Than them, believed the other white guy
When he said he thought I had terrorist ties
Without any proof, no evidence to back him up
But all it took was his rumors to mess it all up
They said they couldn't risk it, had to let me go
No chance to explain, just showed me the door
& that was it, what started it all
That's what I get for chasing that waterfall

٤. Part b: **Life After Death** (My 9/11 survival story)

Setting: Noura flash back to 9/11

Noura:

9/11.
Where were you that day, do you remember?
Can you recall that day in September?
Is it burned in your brain, forever remembered?

It is for me, I'm tied to that day
RELAX FBI, not in THAT way
Hold your judgement so I can explain

Have my own 9/11 story
Kids beware, it's a little gory
الله be with me, to you all the Glory

2001
There between Tower Two & One
Not knowing what's happening, not realizing what's begun

Concrete tumbling all around
Someone jumped & crashed to the ground
His body…now a mangled mound

So close I could see his face
Arms & legs angled strangely out of place
What's happening in this crazy space?

He jumped because the flames were so hot?
Jumping? from up there? was better he thought?
Confused…not knowing what was what

Fleeing the area, seeking my Mom
Didn't know it was planes, thought we were bombed
Really, at ground zero, no one knew what was going on

Only because of ﷲ did I know to run

While others came closer, curious, asking "What's going on?"
Those are the ones that we now mourn

Alhamdulillah, not there when towers crumbled down
Too many lives lost on that hallowed ground
Day marked eternally, forever renowned

2013…call from my Dad
Like clockwork every year cause of that experience we had
I smile, he always calls, only Dad

He says, "Always remember you being saved that day"
"So happy you were ok.
God really answered my prayers that day"

I reply "Only because you came & found us!
Rounded us up like on a school bus
& somehow managed to pick us all up.
He laughs.

Dad was the one who came & got us home
Assuring me, "I'm coming, you're not alone!"
Rescuing us even without cell phones

He battled the chaos & the traffic jams
Drove us to safety in his sturdy van
My Dad, my hero, an incredible man

He called on 9/11 every year
But now that one call is especially dear
6 days later, a daughter's worst fear

Dad's in the hospital not waking up
Doctors can't do anything, his time might be up
Please oh please oh please Dad…wake up!

October 9, 2013 الله called him back up

إِنَّا لِلَّهِ وَإِنَّا إِلَيْهِ رَاجِعُونَ

That 9/11 was the last time we talked
Hospital for 3 weeks but couldn't speak, couldn't walk
Though we prayed…& waited..& watched every movement
like hawks

Usually talked every day…but phone tag THAT week
Wish we'd had more chances to speak

Miss him so much, get *physically* weak

Dad…you know I miss you & your hearty laugh
Your generous heart, palming your face, grabbing your
beard as you laugh
Always ready to give whatever you had

Embodiment of love for others, what you love for self
Always giving from your meager wealth
Without us even knowing! Didn't know you had stealth

Great sense of humor…jokes for days
Told big fish stories in your own way
Made everyone love you & miss you…each & every day

Teacher many times over, not just in your math class
Our time so short, you're gone too fast
Wish that convo wasn't our last

I died a little too that day…2 years before grief fog started
to lift
To return to life, bit by bit
Our fathers…our providers…our men…our gifts!

Nothing compares to a Dad's love for his daughter
Reverse also true for a Dad BY his daughter
Neither time nor age makes it ever falter

Dad…treasure our time & the man you are
Always close, just now *physically* far

Pray الله keeps you wherever you are

& fills your grave with sakeenah…His Divine Light

Time here just a test, Jannah true life
Pray we reunite in highest levels of Paradise
Ameen

o.   **Trial Part One: Opening Remarks** (inspired by:

Redhead Kingpin: Do the Right Thing)

Setting: Courtroom with opposing counsel making opening arguments.

John (opposing counsel):

"Ladies & gentleman, you must do the right thing
In this case, all the facts I'll bring
Protect our country from these terrorists
Once I lay this case out, you'll choose the right verdict"

There he stands tall & arrogant
In his $10,000 suit, so flagrant
Used to juries eating out of the palm of his hand
& the judge lapping it up, allowing him to grandstand

Noura sits quietly waiting for justice
She seems too small to be as dangerous
As reported, "homegrown terrorist", "female Osama"
Barely weighing buck twenty-five, causing so much drama
But then again, Osama wasn't a big dude
& his power had magnitude

Face without emotion as instructed by her lawyer
Though that too works against her
"She doesn't even care! She's a monster!"
"Send her to hell! To her Daddy Osama!"

Noura would laugh at the absurdity
If it wasn't her life destroyed mercilessly
Did they really think they were all related?

One degree away…from Bin Laden?
When facts show…they're more the problem
They are the Fields, Paddocks, & Jacksons
Distracting from the truth by calling us the terrorists
Cliched story repeating, seemingly hopeless
Expected considering who's doing the reporting
Will America ever wake up, stop allowing
Israeli genocide, Palestine Apartheid
Hiding behind…these baseless headlines
Slaughtering innocent people, even children
Stealing land, never theirs to begin with
Islam equals Terrorism, their machination
So easy…to dupe a whole nation
& then the world, basic human rights violations
UN sanctions ignored with elation
Noura wasted her life trying to prove she was "different"
Jaded, she mourned life she could've lived instead

٦. Deen & the Dollar

Setting: Noura in her home meditating

Noura:

Struggling to find my place
Struggling to find my space
When this world judges me by my face

Or what I wear on my head
Or Arabic words I've said
Or that I'll follow a man, happy to be led

But you're independent they say
Why let yourself be treated that way
Stand up for yourself, not in this day!

Unclear why limbs touch the ground when I pray
Or that I CHOOSE to live this way
Defending ourselves everyday is pretty cliché

Don't know why they do what they do
Don't even know why I do what I do
But how do I make this make sense to you

Oh I say "You know how KKK isn't Christianity?"
His eyes are blank, no he doesn't see
Hmm, He's not feeling me

We go back & forth, nothing clicking with him
Why is this so hard, he's not dim
Oh is it just that he wants me to agree with him?

The Block to the
                                   Boardroom

& the story in his mind, already made up
I'm sick of this, could I tell him shut up?
Of course not, then I'd be wrong, man this is messed up
Frustration kicking in, anger about to go wild
but then I take a deep breath & smile
Because I know it's going to take a while

For people to get we're not all the same
We all claim Islam but his actions I can't claim
Don't know why it's done in Islam's name

Won't explain others while still finding myself
Some acts I've done openly, others in stealth
One minute seeking Deen, the next seeking wealth

Seeking the Deen but also the dollar
Do kind of want to be a big baller
What a combo, money & Deen
Change the game, like the world's never seen

Cause there were rich Sahabah with fancy clothes & homes
But others gave away everything they owned
So which actions do I try to clone?

Can I want Oprah money & the Prophets iman?
Is it wrong that this is what I want?
"It's crazy!" my inner demons taunt

Yes الله is my center & all that matters

So…no climbing corporate ladders?
Wait do I hear laughter?

It is funny that I want it all?
I know, it's not really my call
Whatever He decides is how things will fall

Do know that but need to tie my camel
You get me? don't mean to ramble
It's just with my soul I don't want to gamble

Most probably have this worked out
I'm still finding what I'm about
Wanting Deen but also wanting clout

Seeking the Deen but also the dollar
Do kind of want to be a big baller
What a combo, money & Deen
Change the game, like the world's never seen

In hijab but NOT so religious
Just one side of me, this judgement so vicious

Oh الله, how do I fix this?

I'm told I'm just all contradictions
Is it my fault there's no box I fit in?
Cause He made me & only He knows what's written
Like my man will be King & head of our family
& be Presidential cause I'm a First Lady
I know my worth cause my Daddy taught me

So I'll let you drive, together we're growing
I'll follow your lead, my love overflowing
But I'll take back those keys if it's nowhere we're going

Cause I cant stay & be lost but so long

The Block to the
Boardroom

The challenge when you're soft but also strong
The real men know that I'm not wrong

These are my battles as I strive for my purpose

Seeing beauty of الله below the surface

Desperately trying to live in His service

While searching, I'll explore the world
7 continents done, yes I'm that girl
Loving life as adventures unfurl

It's beautiful, this journey I'm on
With His guidance, can't really go wrong
Wherever I land, pray for increased Iman

Seeking the Deen but also the dollar
Do kind of want to be a big baller
What a combo, money & Deen
Change the game, like the world's never seen

V. **John Smith** (inspired by: MC Lyte: Paper Thin)

Setting: Bathroom of corporate office

Noura:

Your whole persona…is paper thin
Overcompensating, doing anything to win
Nothing you say…really even matters
My rejecting you, fragile ego shattered
Spurned, your mission..to bring me down
Spread lies about me all over town
Fueled the hate & Islamophobia
Just cuz I wouldn't give you the time of
Day, or entertain your advances
Reading way more into my glances
Not even my type, need my men more melanated
My success & intelligence you hated
First time, couldn't have what you wanted
White privilege got you believing you're the man &
More important. than this immigrant
But I've got more respect than to get
With you… or any married man
Go back to your wife, be the family man
She thinks you are
when reality is sadder by far
Fake ladies man, nothing without this job
my power you'll never have, given to me by God
white boys' club only reason you in my orbit
without that, we'd have never even met
cuz I'm more talented, got more to offer
Can't handle that, thought you'd get your rocks off

Trapped me in the bathroom, pushed up on me
Working late got you twisted to believe
Could have your way
& you might've, bless that cleaning lady
Don't know what you'd done if she hadn't seen me
& the fear in my eyes
gave me split second to get out, to survive
Though I'd never…be the same
Should've reported you, didn't to protect my name
Cuz gaslighting is real & ruined so many lives

But your time is over, truth & الله on my side

Λ. Love Letter

Setting: Noura in her prayer room in her home

Noura:

used, abused, neglected, rejected by everyone
too Muslim for white America
too "light skinned-ed/good hair/think she cute" for black
too "halwa laikin hindeya" for Arabs
too "Amreekie, kithnee dark hay" for desis
no community...so there is just me

on an island of one
when you have no one
is when your rebirth has begun

no choice but to rely only on الله

crying, praying for death يُا رب

you're what remains الرَّزَّاق

الرَّحِيم

you are my source of health, wealth, & mercy

alone, bleeding & terrified
الْبَصِير, do you see these hot tears I cry?

your world is too hard for me
YOU made me
YOU know how deeply

I care & love
these wounds, these cuts,
please end this يَا رب

not strong enough for the vitriol
my mere presence invokes in all
ٱلسَّمِيع, do you hear me at all?

hated on sight
don't understand my plight
deem me arrogant
without any insight
into me or who I am
know this world a test
MY test can you end?

YOU know my heart
& my true intent
though others believe the worst
ignore my palimpsest
of experiences
moiety of a lover & fighter
yes…I'm a survivor

DOMESTIC VIOLENCE
WHITE PRIVILEGE,
WHITE FRAGILITY,
RACISM,
ISLAMOPHOBIA,
MISOGYNY,
COLONIALISM,

& COLORISM...
compounding on ME
too much to bear

اُلْفَتَّاح

you answer all دعاء

please answer this prayer?

death only refuge I see…
from this pain…
this abuse…
this misery

suicide not an option
because YOU chose this for me
YOU decide when it ends
& that's his response to me…

الله عالم

at least I think:

My child
I made you a WARRIOR!
you ARE
strong enough for these tests
& yes..
you got jokes
how strong you have to be
already Eddie "Hercules, Hercules"

molested so young
cursed your looks
evil it brought out in men
NOT YOUR FAULT
THEY chose to sin

tried to hide
clothed in 3x your size
hidden is not
what I want you to be
hold your head high
walk confidently

haters gonna hate
says more about them.
you're MY truth serum!
exposing what's within
sixth sense
instead of "I see dead people"
you see their energy
unleashing their hurt on you,
unfairly
& that's heavy

don't let Shaitan
make you forget
the immediate love you get
from those souls
with whom you connect
ones most concerned
not w/ this life but the next

anger brings out your best work
why won't I let
love inspire you instead?
no husband yet
write from your heart
& your head
you'll marry when I decide
for right now
you're only mine

artist & engineer
math is its own poetry
formulas create magic bc of me

your dark humor?
also from me
as is your lineage
of story tellers, mathematicians, & yogis
started from Asia
started from thee
columbus sought YOUR country
for its spices & jewels
crown jewels stolen from you
when they ruled

The Block to the
Boardroom

now you see
how far he was off
nowhere near India
but white privilege…
he just named it wrong
you are the India he sought

gave you beauty
in the physical form
so your message is received
not from
your outer...
but whether you have humility

اَللّٰهُمَّ كَمَا حَسَّنْتَ خَلْقِى فَحَسِّنْ خُلُقِى

your دعاء daily

made you, yes
but man has free will
a choice
you decide
how to use your voice
your wit
your power
your genius
your beauty
carefully? or weapons brandished harshly?

thin line
between arrogance & confidence
you show me your stance

جنّةُ فردوس

not for those
faint of faith
you must be awake
serve only ME
not money or fame
suffer poverty

I am المعز

المُذِل

you have free will
I give & take away
cannot claim

جنّةُ unless you stay

content with this life
regardless of strife…
valleys of darkness…
to heights I let you climb
child of mine

my beloved
you are not wicked
or cast away
I am with you every day

The Block to the
Boardroom

incomprehensible, my tests
you'll ask me in جَنّة

"break it down
why did children suffer
why'd you do that to me?"

knowing in جَنّة

no concerns like these…
everyone only happy

your job?
your purpose?
is not to understand
because how can
you understand
the things I create?
engineer! studied gravity & physics
but can you levitate?

I decide
I am ٱلأَوَّل

الاخر

my love for you is everywhere
closer to you
than your jugular vein
stand tall
rely on me
you CAN stand the rain

The Block to the
Boardroom

warriors cry too
your pillow nightly soaked
because you are woke
every day you fight
execute my plan

your judgement will NOT be دُنْيا success

but how you stand

prayed for purpose
never said it would be easy
only I know your true destiny.

Noah with the ark
building alone
to close ALL the gaps
education, wealth, and wellness
corruption you expose

like your boy,
might not change the world
but might be the spark
for next boy or girl

each one of you
is a part of my plan.
drops in an ocean…
tsunami when I put you in motion
only worry about me
MY pleasure
MY protection
& you cannot go wrong.

The Block to the
Boardroom

I will hold you strong
even if the whole world plots against you
unless I decide
you cannot be harmed

peacock
not made to blend
olympian
kiddie pool not for you
your arena is much bigger
I decreed that for you

only I know
how much you can take
شياطين tests you

yours is my soul to take

trust in me
& I will bring you through
I PROMISE this to you
hold fast to the fact that
I...L...YOU

even if everything & everyone fall away

يا الله !

يا مهيمن !

يا ودود!

In your name I pray

٩. دعاء **Up** (inspired by: Tupac: Hit em up)

Setting: TED conference

Noura:

[HOOK]
Check your hearts, for who you rock

For me, it's الله, الرَّزَّاقُ

Don't @ me with no bs
Serve Him alone, this life...just a test

دعاء Up

First off, check your heart & the clic you claim
Eastside till I die but Pac my man
Genius with a message but screwed in life
Shot 5 times... dead at 25

Lover but his...heart was ripped
Went from Dear Mama to that BS
We keep on going
no money in our schools
Steady climbing, not becoming a tool
Breakin the rules
Could we please a...
Higher Power, all this will leave ya
When time is up
All this beef
Nipsey assasinated helpin the streets

Pray he's at peace
Inventin wars, we need peace
Another angel killed by the life
Life cut short, who knew…heights he'd climb
Young kings & queens, no reason being killed
System working flawlessly just how it's built

[HOOK]
Check your hearts, for who you rock

For me, it's الرَّزَّاقُ, الله

Don't @ me with no bs
Serve Him alone, this life…just a test

دعاء Up

Need دعاء, more prayers though

It hurts, pain just won't stop
Gotta think…before we hit back
Odds against us, stacked
Whiteprivilege in this life
Always feelin trapped
No accidents cops murderin us
Continue to keep hurtin us
Shaitan's attacks
& no justice serving us
Country built on slaves' backs then immigrants
Corruption through all…all the ranks
But they getting weaker as we see the picture is bigger
Katherine Johnson, now we see the Hidden Figures
Once we get empowered only then will we flower

Instead of being sour & the time will be ours
Dua Up

[HOOK]
Check your hearts, for who you rock

For me, it's الله, الرَّزَّاقُ

Don't @ me with no bs
Serve Him alone, this life...just a test

دعاء Up

Keep it real, who profit from penitentiary steel
Wars, sons & daughters getting killed, keep ya eyes open
Follow the money, who NRA pays, guns' smoking
Drugs & misery they don't want us to fly
Tired of seeing my fam...out here dying
Driven by money, this ain't funny to me
Biden out here coddling the wealthy elite
Shout out to Chamillionaire
Helping make more melanated millionaires
Lifting each other up is what it's all about
But it's hard to do, if we don't have our house
In order, it's going to...take a while
But my faith, His mercy makes me smile
So let's get ourselves straight
Educate, spread love & stop self hate
Dua Up

From N-e-w Jers
Bronx is where I learned
Don't start none, won't be none...don't get hurt

The Block to the
Boardroom

Now check this scenario
Ally, don't mistake it though
Verbal assassin…you'll hit the floor
Before you even know, I'm out the door
Not coked up or doped up
Around it never smoked up

الله made me genius, not stupid

J.Bourne you, lucky just words I'm shootin
Came at me, shootin & pollutin
The vibe. Cuz me from the block?
Unleashed, can't be stopped
Left that life, to go up another notch
In Deen…keep Shaitan locked

الله knows my heart, don't fit in your box

Fear Him alone, care about His props
Haters you can all…kick rocks

١. **Trial Part Two: Betrayals** (inspired by: Nas: Made You Look)

Setting: Courtroom with Mike on the stand.

Jeremy (Noura's attorney):

Mike took the stand, swore to tell the truth
Then lied through the whole thing, speaking on cue
Saying exactly what they wanted him to say
Couldn't meet her eyes, didn't once look her way
Forgotten all the hours spent with his kid
Wouldn't be where he was if she hadn't him
Thought they were friends but clearly not
When he sold her out without a second thought
Claiming he never really knew her deceit
He's the victim, conned him so artfully
Apparently, that was her master plan all along
Haven't people had enough of this, old tired song?
"I thought she was one of the good ones!
How was I supposed to know?"
White fragility, he's bamboozled by her show
For 15 years?! Then she's a damn good actress
How does she defend against the sheer nonsense
If so diabolical, why would she stop here?
Would've conquered the world, not stopped at C-suite tier
Her persona had you shook? yeah she'll do that
Cuz she's that fierce, don't be mad

[HOOK]

They shootin, uh, made me look
Didn't think they'd lie but then they are crooks
Her own fault…for trustin em
That's cool…won't happen again

His lies continue as he spins his tales
Jury trusting him, good white boy from Yale
White fragility & privilege even has us confused
Thinking we're doing good, even though they still choose
When we eat, if we're allowed at the table
& when we're out, doesn't matter if we're able
To do all they can & so much more

I've had enough, time to settle the score

The Block to the
Boardroom

\\. **Black Love/Khadijah** (inspired by: D'Angelo:

Brown Sugar)

Setting: Courtroom where Khadijah's husband calls. She answers & gives him a quick update.

Khadijah:

Let me tell you about this couple
As cute as can be
They been together for eternity
3 kids & they still crazy in love
That kind of love
Only comes from above
Best friends…always got each other's back
Don't tolerate any kind of attack
Brown sugar babes
So crazy in love they don't know how to behave

[HOOK]
They're so in love, brown sugar
They're so in love, brown sugar

Always united, take care of each other
Beautiful example for our sisters & brothers
They way they look
into each others eyes
You'd think they were…hypnotized

High school sweethearts, married oh so young

Even after 19 years, they still having fun
He worships the ground on which she walks
& she listens intently every time he talks

[HOOK]
He's her King & she's His Queen
Won't let anyone come in.in between
If you ask em, how they do it
They say, it's simple no secret
Respect each other, always communicate
Even when you argue, don't do it with hate
Genuinely like each other
accept others faults even as they grow together

[HOOK]
Brown sugar babes, they get high off each other, don't know
how to behave
They're so in love, brown sugar
They're so in love, brown sugar

١٢. Muslim Representative

Setting: Corporate office with Noura & her mentor

Noura:

Noura, as my only Muslim friend
Have a question, your ear will you lend?
Cringed not knowin what to say
He's going to want me to speak for all Muslims today
When how can anyone...really do that?
2 billion of us, will they ever get that?
Not monolithic, everyone's practice their own
I'm a prime example, by some Muslims I'm disowned
Too liberal for some, too conservative for others
Cuz I wear hijab but also work with all brothers
Around men literally all day
& criticized for living my life this way

[HOOK]
I am an Around the Way Girl
That's Who I Am Honestly
I am an Around the Way Girl
That's Who I Am Honestly

Sun streamed through his corner office
Four years, from mentor to friendship
How could I possibly be his only Muslim friend?
Cuz of where he lives? His time? How does he spend?
Senior VP, Republican & affluent

The Block to the
                                Boardroom

That's the group that he represents
But that's by choice, he could venture out
Learn more about others, if he branched out
But he chooses to stay in his little bubble
Expecting me to be human Muslim Wiki, this'll get me in trouble
How I practice is unique to just me
But if I don't answer him, will his ignorance be on me?
Telling him to Google it, is that cheap or petty?
Damn it, why is this on me?

[HOOK]
I am an Around the Way Girl
That's Who I Am Honestly
I am an Around the Way Girl
That's Who I Am Honestly

His White Privilege lets him believe
This is ok, anything else he can't even conceive
Of course it's my job to educate him on Islam
On top of proving myself, working harder for what I want
Than any of his white boy friends, that's the rule
Be twice as good, never lose your cool
The literal intersection of religion, race, & gender
But don't talk about it, that's not in the
Corporate Handbook, so don't bring it up
We'll just assume everything about you, suck it up
Harder to wear religion on my head than heart on my sleeve
How do I respond to him & do it tactfully
I took a deep breath before I responded
Sole Muslim friend brings responsibility I never wanted

[HOOK]
I am an Around the Way Girl
That's Who I Am Honestly
I am an Around the Way Girl
That's Who I Am Honestly

The Block to the
Boardroom

٣١. **Sara** (inspired by: Salt N Pepa: Express Yourself)

Setting: Sara's modest apartment home with her Baba watching TV & her mother cooking.

Sara:

Israeli soldiers killed another one
This time a nurse named Raza Ashraf
Baba parked in his usual spot
Listening to the latest, all fraught
With death & despair, what's reported
Sara almost immune to the war, gore, &
Apartheid…in Palestine
She cares but death is always on her mind
Became a nurse just to please her Baba
To fulfill the dream of Auntie Jamillah
Even though blood made her nauseous & still does
How long can she live her life not doing what she loves
Which she wasn't even sure what that was
Which is why she continued this crazy charade

[HOOK]
Express Yourself, how does one do that baby?
Express Yourself, who do I even want to be?
Express Yourself, what do I want to do baby
Express Yourself, who am I? am I anybody?

Baba never talked about it, much too painful
Sara knew little, sole survivor of the missile

Only because he'd not been home
Sent to find safe passage, venturing out alone
His Baba killed just the previous week
At Israeli soldier's whim, & havoc unleashed
Gentle man, never hurt anyone
Life cut too short by child with massive gun
Then Baba's head of the house at just age nine
No time to grieve, there was no time
While he was out, another missile hit
Baba knocked off his feet, thrown by the force of it
He ran back, praying it missed his home
But his prayers unanswered, found the charred bodies
thrown
Limbs everywhere, couldn't tell who was who
Part of him died that day with his youngest sister, only two

[HOOK]
Express Yourself, how does one do that baby?
Express Yourself, who do I even want to be?
Express Yourself, just tell me what to do baby
Express Yourself, who am I? am I anybody?

Baba & Jamillah, always close, now he sainted her
Wouldn't let anything negative taint her
Memory or who he believed her to be
In Baba's memory, she was always compliant
Though Sara heard of her wild streak, actually defiant

Sara tried to live her Baba's memory
Protect him from more pain & tried to be
Smart, dutiful, & always perfect

The Block to the
                        Boardroom

Losing herself in the process
& now feeling completely boxed in
His high expectations impossible to meet
Working a job she hated every day a huge feat
Disappointing him would break her heart along with his
She refused to be the one to do that to him

[HOOK]
Express Yourself, how does one do that baby?
Express Yourself, who do I even want to be?
Express Yourself, just tell me what to do baby
Express Yourself, who am I? am I anybody?

૬ ૧. **Isabella** (inspired by: Roxanne: Roxanne's Revenge)

Setting: Isabella's home arguing with her husband.

Isabella:

My best friend, my beloved, my Christian husband
A cheater, a liar, who broke our vows &
Didn't think twice about destroying my heart
& now our life is torn apart
Life we built so carefully
So-called Christian friends nowhere to be seen
Somehow my fault, drove you to her
Wasn't a good wife cause I didn't adore
Your every move, worship ground you walked on
Irony is I did & that's what you stomped on
More I bowed down, more disgusted you became
Love impossible when I lived in such shame
Allowed disrespect, thought that was love
Verbal abuse like fists in velvet gloves
Excusing your behavior, he didn't mean that
Calling me fat
With this gut, how can I attract
Him? So I lost the weight
Our sex life never been great

But then it was my nose, & then my laugh
Everything I did put him on the war path
Lost myself in him, ignored my own needs
How did I get here? & how do I get free?

Daily prayer to God, He always answers
& when He did, things couldn't move faster
Proof of infidelity fell in my lap
Wasn't looking, almost made me laugh
Sexting, really? This is what you're doing?
Not worried about reputation being ruined?
Our friends knew...& never told me?
Godmother to their kids but this couldn't tell me?
Watched me run myself into the ground for years
& how many nights did they watch me shed tears

Thank God my love for Him is stronger than this
Cuz if it wasn't, the entire faith I'd dismiss
As fake, hypocritical, & complete waste of time
But your unctuous faith won't destroy mine
Don't understand His plan but Know He loves me
Put my trust in Him, know He'll guide me
Through this just like He's always done
Pray to Him & His Only Begotten Son

Please Lord help me, heal my heart
remove the anger don't let bitterness start
to take root because it will destroy me
& let me find the love YOU want for me

Thought it was him but you have another plan
Will not be destroyed by some man
Want a family, one day, a daughter
But won't let anyone else hurt me or slaughter
My spirit or dampen my shine
Please Lord heal my spirit, know it takes time.

I'll try to be patient, please help me through
This I pray, put my trust in you
Protect me from the devil in the form of man
In Jesus name I pray, Amen

The Block to the
Boardroom

٥١. **Appropriating April** (inspired by: Lauryn Hill: Lost Ones)

Setting: Noura's home yoga studio. Flashback after April takes the stand.

Noura:

It's funny how money change a situation
I send an email you send a cop with a gun
White people blowing things out of proportion
When all I did was ask for a refund
For a trip that sucked! That was no fun
Supposed to be one of rejuvenation
Instead filled with discrimination
You telling me you're Polish when I tell you what I want
That's not the same, you're really too much
Then telling me "be careful" how I speak of mistreatment
Ridiculous that cop spurred you on
Your racism won't get this one
Call yourself a healer but clearly you ain't one

Appropriating April, you dead wrong
Stole yoga from me, colonization
Gaslighting me when I'm owed a refund
Hope your Cuba trip really gets no one

Appropriating April, you messed with the wrong one
I send an email, you send a cop with a gun
Your privilege has gotchu messed up

Stop your gaslighting cuz I'm not the one

No one else, should have this done
So I'll speak out for other melanated ones
& hope to protect next generations
Past ones too, Emmett Till, a young one
Beaten & killed cuz of another white one
Your racism killed too many of our sons
Philando, Eric, Trayvon, Bonham Jean
Daughters too, Sandra Palestinian Rezan
So many to name, too many Lost Ones
Where I come from, don't start none won't be none
Brought this on yourself & now you're done
Shut down your company, get some education
Read a book, Sue's Microaggressions
& "White Fragility", learn & then come
Back to me, actually don't cause I'm done

Hope your trips get cancelled & your company done
Cause you done messed with the wrong one
Asbury police, what's the explanation
But don't tell me, tell my representation
Breaking the law instead of upholding em
Law is on my side, for me, this will be won

Appropriating April, you messed with the wrong one
I send an email, you send a cop with a gun
Your privilege has gotchu messed up
Stop your gaslighting cuz I'm not the one [repeat]

Speaking for all those killed for no reason
Too many, too many, too many lost ones

The Block to the
                                    Boardroom

Trying to trigger me, make me violent
Use my words, my ammunition
Not giving in to this intimidation
Your white fragility, bright like the sun
So racist, claiming you're not one
Asbury police, can't believe what you've done
This is wild beyond imagination
Hid your white hood & fooled me once
But now April you are done

Appropriating April, you messed with the wrong one
I send an email, you send a cop with a gun
Your privilege has gotchu messed up
Stop your gaslighting cuz I'm not the one [repeat]

٦١. White privilege playing tricks on me – Ode to

Corporate America (inspired by: Mind Playing Tricks On Me)

Setting: Noura escorted out of her office building by security.

Noura:

At night, I can't sleep, I toss & turn
White faces scaring me, won't let me earn
My living…always holding me down
Why you always mad, turn that frown upside down
Smile! Don't be the angry Muslim
What? No, we don't like him
Better than you, don't be paranoid
Just cuz he's a member of the white boys
Club, we're more comfortable with him
That doesn't mean that you also can't win
Work harder, tolerate their advances
You'll shut up if you want advancement
Don't be too loud, don't be too quiet
Not too independent, see you're not trying
Don't be too ugly or too pretty
Not too fat or too skinny
Speak up in meetings but not too much
Just the right amount & also bring us lunch
Take notes won't you, you're such a doll
Don't get emotional, don't bust our balls
John stole your idea? Pretty sure it was his.

You said it first? Don't be like this

[HOOK]
Gaslighting playin tricks on me
White fragility playin tricks on me
White privilege playin tricks on me

It's not attractive, that's why you're still single
& why you all covered? Come on let em jingle
Heard you were from "around the way"
Call you ghetto, disrespect you all day
But be a team player, help John succeed
We'll recognize you, of course, indeed
Act like one of the boys but watch our glass egos
Didn't you know, this is how it goes?
How do you think Becky got VP?
She knew how to get down on her knees
What do you mean she won't let you pray
Told you move Jumaa to another day?
You're C-suite, won't tolerate that
Not on my watch, to the bottom of that, stat
Best place to work, Fortune, #73
Of course…we value diversity
Geez, why'd you bring this to me?
This is why we don't…let you in the room
Don't belong…in the boardroom
Only here to check a box
Six figures means your soul we bought

[HOOK]
Gaslighting playin tricks on me
White fragility playin tricks on me

The Block to the
Boardroom

White privilege playin tricks on me

Only want diversity when it's convenient
Time off to pray would be too lenient
Our plantation, we make the rules
Our downfall, letting you in school
Damn that Brown …screwed us for sure
Education equalizes, settles the score
We all know, you're smarter than us
That's why we want you in the back of the bus
Systemic oppression our only hope
Blocking wellness so you can't cope
But even then, you persist
Mind games & torture, you resist
To stand here & challenge me
Last ditch effort: label you public enemy
Number one, ruin your reputation
Should've stayed quiet, known your place &
Took the abuse, you got HR involved
You're now a problem we have to solve
Cuz now you have…the grounds to sue
We'll make sure to ruin you
400 lawyers, set you up, spit you out
Leave the Black Card, we'll escort you out

The Block to the
Boardroom

٧١. Lifestyles of the weak & the shameless (inspired by:

Lost Boys: Lifestyles of the Rich & the Famous)

Setting: Noura in her home reflecting on Glock

Everybody frontin' don't give a damn

Straight from Boogie Down comes this dude named
Glock
Everyone knew Glock, he ran the block
Controlled it all, real life Neeno Brown
'cept he won't flip even if ish went down
Glock and his fam, on a street won't say the cross
Let's just say it crossed
w/ Grand Concourse

Started slinging cuz that's all we knew
What everybody did, that's how we grew
Up, DNA 100% thug dudes
Don't pity them, they will straight body you
Realest dudes you'll ever meet
Happy he chose me to holla at, that night in Jersey
on street
1st letter P

That was the spot…we'd hang after school
Oblivious to his being some roughneck dude
Just saw he had kind eyes, thought he was cute
Plus Glock ran…"construction" line on me
When asked what he did…for money

Tough as he was, to me he was only sweet
intelligent and patient too every time we'd meet
Gentleman, always opened my door,
Walked street side…always kept me warm
Reeboks every color…cuz of him
Even dope violet ones, man I loved them

Those kicks & Glock…made me cool
Kept female AND male tricks from hurtin me at that
corny school

After Dad, Glock only one who had my back
But Glock's approach was wickedy wack
Never stepped to Dad…as a man
To ask him for…his daughter's hand
And Dad, my King, wasn't having it
Not for his fave, his heart
Swore he'd forever keep us apart
Dad taught me, Queen deserved better
Schooled me on diff between compromise & settle

Being naïve, didn't know what to do
Loved being his, that everyone knew
Don't mess with her, that's Glock's girl
My King! Chose me as Queen, ran that world
Eff Bonnie & Clyde, not dead young in a gun whirl

Dad & Glock, real men, taught me the game, street
rules
Now run those street rules
legally in boardrooms

The Block to the
Boardroom

Never snitch…know how to move
Stay low…always…keep your cool
Don't rush…but don't linger,
Keep it hidden, finger on the trigger
Mind ya business, move with stealth
Be quiet one & stack your wealth

Was and will forever be
HBIC
Stay that, that's Head Boss, all me
Other word, not my vernacular
Love being Queen, life spectacular
Was my vernacular
See…what had happened was
Penta-lingual & street is native one
Chameleon
Can talk white if need be to get the job done
Alhamdulillah, I rise above

Fake brauds quake…when they see me
Mad my hair real & they can't be me
Scream "Go back to your country"
When in reality
Only Indigenous belong more than me
Let's not forget this country
Founded on quest for India, other words, ME

Some dudes…they fraud too
No game, fumble trying to holla at you
Insecure…cuz I'm out their league
Not my fault, they can't reach the Queen

Don't shoot that shot, no shot with me
And don't test me…you will be done
Bodied before you…even see the gun

Of course, officer gotta permit for this
Paperwork tight, go and ask Gladys
You know over, over, at the Precinct
All here and that's the diff
between me & Glock, I stay legit

Glock loved me & almost got me killed
Crack house shooting, blood spilled
Glock did cover me &
Protect me
with his own body
Never should've been there, actually
inshAllah violent death not my destiny

الله always with me, protects me

He watches over…children and fools
No longer in high school
Grown now, child no longer claim

الله knows fool I could never claim

Glock not in right company
Almost gang raped, led by his boy K
Punk, said Glock gave his ok
Knew that wasn't true
Glock would never but he kept him around through
The years and snake dudes

Make snake moves
K being cut off and out, long overdue

Didn't tell Glock until years later
Painful to discuss, buried it, graveyard
Glock didn't say:

"That's horrible! Sorry I brought that to your life"
Or "sorry, bc of me you almost died"
Or "sorry, bc of me almost didn't graduate"
Or "sorry, bc of me your self-esteem deflated"
Or "sorry, bc of me everybody hated
On you. From cops to other brauds I effed & then
lied to you"

He said "Can't believe K did that to ME."
To him, really?
Always about him, when it almost destroyed me
That life resurfaces nightmares
about me back there
Calling Glock for help and he's not there

Glock's a King still playing boy games
Don't know what'll it take for him to change
Real men run their own kingdom
Not content at their brother's throne
No place to call their own
Mom's house still main home

Men will treat you how they treat their Mom
Treat you the same, don't be surprised from
Endure the pain and drama

Kinda have issue w/ these Mommas
For not raising men, staying in the drama
Accountability never taught
Never their fault
To man up, take responsibility
Bc their men not around
Turn their sons into man of the house & that's how
Cycle repeats, pray we break it

That's why I protect my nieces & nephews
From that life & my brother too
That punk dude
Took from me for years and then turned on me too

Refuse to be…
another stat
Like Nipsey, Pac, all the others that
killed in…senseless violence
Too much ish to do with this genius

That's right, GENIUS
Claiming it
didn't stutter…finally clear on this

Unlike Mileva Maric
No dude ever Einstein this
Nobel prize winning thesis
wasn't even his
Sucker men *don't* appreciate
Steal your ish and try claim it
For their own but that's ok

The Block to the
Boardroom

الْبَصِيرُ ,السَّمِيعُ

Bump the haters, in His name I pray
Penta rev streams
All run professionally
Kindness is not weakness…don't test me
Corporate game, still street rules
Especially for crusty white privilege dudes

Factory burned down? Eff you pay me
Tough month, aww…eff you pay me?
Wife on your nerves? Double eff you pay me
Only get worse if you don't have my money
That's a YOU problem, not a problem for me

Degrees enhance my street ed
Doc title real unlike Special Ed
3 degrees, 6 certs and counting

ال حمد الله

الله keeps my stacks mounting

Even with…my pedigree
crusty white fragility
try to play me
Call me sweetie
When I'm the one LEADING
The whole company meeting

Maaaaaan, jihad every day

Why الله made me مسلم,

The Block to the
Boardroom

why I pray
[laughs] Don't even know
Narrow escape from that label on their toe

لا تغضب

…my everyday mantra
Cuz I really, really don't…wanna
Catch a case…over some fools
Too important, got ish to do

Been decades Glock, cool to reminisce
Hope you know…how much I miss
You and us! How much you meant to this
Nerdy quiet girl, jumped for ish
Outta my control, Hated cuz "light skinned-ed long haired girl"

Much love Glock for showing me
What it means to be
real man that commands respect quietly
Tried to protect me from your violence
But also…took advantage
Carried weight through
Not cuz I wanted to
Snuck in my bookbag
Next to math books
Me too oblivious to
Warning signs, his own fam warned me
Shout out to RJ and Double T
Dummy me, refused to listen
too in love to pay attention

To what's cooking in the kitchen

Visited for every one of his bids
My "bid" was college
& Glock never *once* visited
Didn't get to know me, or where I was
Effed up when your King don't reciprocate love

At that time, looking for love
In ALL the wrong places

الله is the One

As Ali realized الله is the greatest

لا حول ولاقوة إلا بالله

No hard feelings, أعوذ بالله

No grudges, not that person
Laser focused, to be in His service

السَّلاَمُ الْوَدُودُ

Better love than any dude
شياطين deceives, they think punishment escaped
الْعَدْلُ sentence carries most weight

نفسي demands everything now

الله decides, now or later

That's a nope, not seeing me later

Protect myself now
Any…means…necessary
Emotional cigarette, killing me slowly
Know Glock's not what's best for me
100%, unequivocally

الله has a higher plan for me

Glock's choices are his
While I detest that life for him
Never have & *never will* judge him

الله watches over us

الحمد لله He loves us

Pray Glock gets out the game
Away from those crooked cops, RKing-ed his brain

Beg Glock to reflect
What's…his part in it?
Who put him in that position
to be chased by them?
Glock…the LCD
no, no, not LSD
That's the #mathNerd in me

The Block to the
Boardroom

LCD, lowest common denominator
Love yourself enough to want greater

Stop with the revisionist history
Crazy editing, reality TV
His world, never his fault
Do you booboo, not volunteering for more assaults

Maybe, if Glock survives another 10
Stays alive…and out the penn
Maybe we'd have a chance?
But if I'm being honest
Know that last night was our last dance

Only الله knows…when it's our time

إن شاء الله making most of mine

جنّة فردوس in my crosshairs

Pray we reunite up there

In service to Him
He is my goal
جنّة VIP, Dad's waiting for his little girl

Asked nicely before: leave me alone, don't come
around me
If in some cruel twist of irony
We happen to be
In the same room and you see me?
Walk away, don't sidle next to me

The Block to the
Boardroom

No longer asking
Know what I'm carrying

Forever love & be grateful to Glock
Protected me, taught me a lot
But coming back to the block?
That I'm not

الله saved me..from that life

Forward movement, not same mistake twice
Birthed amongst violence

With الله always rise from the ashes

If you believe nothing else, believe this

Maybe in another lifetime we'll meet again
But until then
Won't get this love, this heart again
No more distractions from my purpose
Always in my prayers & my heart
Will send love & دعاء from afar

جنّة فردوس, VIP جنّة

MY True Goal...إن شاء الله my destiny

Pray Glock stays protected from one above
السلام عليكم my first love

The Block to the
Boardroom

Λ\.   **Trial Part Three: Closing Remarks** (inspired by: Blacksheep: Choice Is Yours)

Setting: Courtroom for closing arguments.

Jeremy (Noura's attorney):

It's almost done yo, it's almost done
It's almost done yo, it's almost done
It's almost done yo, it's almost done
It's almost done yo, it's almost done
This or that

Who's the guilty, where's the guilty?
Presented our case, it's really a clear story
Terrorist mad that she's discovered
Bringing us to trial, not accepting it's over
Accusing us?! that's laughable
Our only mistake? thinking she's laudable
Her accusations really an affront
To our fine company, what does she want?
She needs to go back to her own country
Maybe that's allowed in that ****hole country
Cuz all of you, you all know
The right thing to do here, end this show

We have friends in high places, this is beneath us
You know we're right, you have to believe us
We're the patriarchy, you'll never bring us down
Fall in line, you should know that by now

Only one outcome, we're good white boys
You know this, the choice is yours

[HOOK]
You could side with us, or you could side with that
You could side with us, or you could side with that
You could side with us, or you could side with that
Think you'll side with us, cuz our checks are fat

Who's the guilty, where's the guilty?
Have to dismiss, even though our case is weak
So what if she has proof of discrimination
White privilege is the foundation
of this nation
Therefore please ignore
All the facts of this case
& side with us, that's what we're sayin
Dismiss this without further delay &
Let us get back to printing money &
We know we'll get off easy
Because we always do, that's our history
Anytime someone fights us, we knock them
Down because bullies can't be stopped &
Never was it done before that we had to pay
For our bullying & we won't today

Billion dollar company, all over the globe
Deep pockets we'll fight forever & we control
All the politicians so give up now
Fall in line, you should know that by now

[HOOK]
You could side with us, or you could side with that
You could side with us, or you could side with that
You could side with us, or you could side with that
Think you'll side with us, cuz our checks are fat

Jury, jury, with people so fine
Know what to do, it's the end of her line
Protect us…from her attacks
Send her back, send her back, send her back

Jury's back, let's reconvene
Baited breaths, it's quite the chaotic scene
She's the outcast, thrown in the gutter
Though she stood strong, never once did she stutter
When defending herself & her character
The verdict will decide if that will matter
Her eloquence worked in her favor
She said this imbroglio won't dissuade her
Because this is what melanated people do
Keep fighting even when odds are against you
Who talks like that, growing up how she did?
Public school kids don't come out like this
Landmark case just being brought to trial
She refused to settle despite their bribes
She wanted her day in court & at least she got that
Quiet down, it's almost time
"We the jury find..."

The Block to the
                                    Boardroom

٩١. Slam: Leave Boys to Their Toys (inspired by: Onyx: Slam)

Leave boys with their toys
Real men only please, no boys
It's another one, trying to come
At me wrong cuz I'm quiet one
boys will be boys, why I don't eff with them
Only deal with Kings, real Alpha men
Who recognize a Queen when in her presence
Show the proper respect & respect will be given

No response to "girl" "baby" or "sweetie"
You don't know me
Nicknames reserved for DJT
Or my King, my hubby
Privilege for you to even…eff with me
Sultana, Reina those work too
language don't matter, it's the meaning booboo

You & me, we not the same
Be careful…when you say my name
Put RESPECT ON IT or keep it out your mouth
Calmed down since I…moved down south
Don't get it twisted still rep the Boogie Down
And Jersey
Don't eff with me
Stop trying to be me, don't have my pedigree
Haters only come at me if they ain't Queens

Or Kings, trying to pass the blame
That's a nope return to sender, returned unclaimed
Woosah…to keep myself cool
But Daddy…ain't raise no file
Not the rah rah…wile out chick
I'm Queen dispatches the pawn & now your throat slit
Clutching at your neck to stop the blood
Slowly realizing…your time is done
On notice say goodbye…to your loved ones
Won't have time later
Salaam for now, we'll be seeing you later

٠٢. **Get Em High** (inspired by: Kanye: Get 'Em High)

That was tight but it needed this female
To really set it off and balance the male
Energy which was hot as f----
With this woman, coulda really, really pushed it up
Past, your normal orbit
Don't play me to the left, not your average chick
Actually, not even a chick
I'm the Queen with
The dope lyrics

Degrees, stacks, and stage presence too
Dad called me a Queen since I was like 2
And that's how I move,
Don't like it? not a Me problem, that's a problem for
you

Not a King? yeah, you'll feel threatened
Cuz you can only handle women, if they're submissive
I can be that, in the bedroom, playing a role
But out in the real world, take that ish and go
To someone else
Cuz I ain't the one
What the Bronx say? Don't Start None...
Won't Be None

Artist AND a motherfreaking engineer
Linguist, Fortune 100, C-suite career
Rock the Yankees cap and the stilettos too
But only for the right one & booboo that ain't you

The Block to the
                                                                  Boardroom

Can I burn? Feed you more ways than one
My intellect and creativity have you speaking in
tongues
Calm your excitement tho...only for my husband
Little boys get mad when I reject them
call me a lesbian

Whatever booboo for your ego to cope
Forget planet, different galaxies and yours is broke
You mad? Fly on an elephant
All you are...is a mild annoyance
Not gonna...ruin my day
The way I rock, either love you or you don't exist in
my brain

١٢. End of Her Story (inspired by: Slick Rick: Children's Story)

Setting: Courtroom where Jeremy (Noura's attorney) is making closing remarks

Jeremy (Noura's attorney):

Turn her body over, where's the gun?
Like Tamir, there never was one
Her bullets…were her words
This Is America, only violence gets heard
Microaggressions, unwanted advances
Bullets hitting us, superheroes we catch them
Just cuz we hold them & don't spray
Don't mean we can't…make you pay

Shoot all those bullets right back at you
Then we'll have your ear like we tried to do
But you don't listen
Shut us down
Criticized us, shift focus, wow
That's a nope, nice gaslighting
Tried to make us wrong for fighting
For what's right, caring for each other
Don't have to be Black for Black Lives to Matter
Like Palestine, lives being shattered
Brothers & sisters in humanity
Being killed oh so casually

Noura:

& please stop, Permit Patties
Out here, wasting police time
Then they don't come for an actual crime
Or when they do, they're too damn shook
Scared to death, scared to book
Or even let me file a report
Just like Pac, Me Against the World
Defend myself if I have to
Don't think this won't, come back to you

I'm Muslim: warrior for Joy
Won't stop me even with all your ploys

الله has my back, Only One I need

Won't let me hide & run away weak

Protect MYSELF, any means necessary
Brought old me out, warned you she's scary
The Hulk, you made her mad
Verbal Assassin, no more BS will she have

Unleashed, dead before you hit the ground
Metaphorically effed your brain before you even made a sound
Tightness, feeling in your chest
Are my words taking away your breath
Seizing you, it's cardiac arrest
Just cuz I let it slide a few times
Thought you'd keep going…nope, it's your time

Times Up, Me too, Me A Million

Don't be a pervert & I won't hurt your feelings

I'm a survivor, ﷲ is in control

Pray for Him to save my soul
& Guard me as I speak out
Not just me, the word is out
NOT going to…walk all over us
Tried to screw us, now you're the one f---

Let this be
Your last memory
Brought this on yourself, really not on me

Told you & told you, don't say you weren't warned
Hope your will is ready, cuz now you'll be mourned

Epilogue: Know ﷲ Loves Me

Setting: Noura in green room waiting to go on stage to accept award for reaching Forbes Billionaires List

Noura:

Introvert

I usually have that laid back, chill vibe
When I sit back & think, have deep deep thoughts
What is my purpose, what exactly have I brought
To people's lives, what's the meaning of life?

Only ﷲ knows how long we'll all be alive

So much trauma & painful strife
Still joyful tho, tryin to keep it together
As cops harass me, still thug life forever
Cuz repercussions little infants see
not limited to black community
Those cops that grow up, think they're bad with a gun
Until they're recorded, now they on the run
Don't want witnesses to these modern day lynchings
& then we got shaitan, out here pimping
Little black girls, predators like rkelly
Hell his place…gotta be
That doc, so painful to watch
Yet so grateful to Dream for the light it brought
Back to it, shame we ain't listen before
Believe Women even when we are poor
Especially then, that's who gets preyed on

Slow Genocide singin bout girls he preyed on

Back to الله purpose, why I'm here

What else are we doing if on that we're not clear?
Tell people I'm on…some next level faith
Don't care if they laugh or even hate
His judgement is my only concern
Don't care if His pleasure is not what you yearn

Not judging, leave that up to الله

Cuz He knows, I have my share of flaws
Zero patience, no tolerance for bullies
Come correct to me or keep it…movin please

See whachu got twisted is I'm actually…an introvert
Not thinking about you, not trying to convert
You or anyone else…for that matter
Just bringing attention to Black Lives Matter
& other important causes, Palestine, TimesUp
Cuz I see how this world..is really so messed up

& how I'm different is that I ponder & surmise
Like a bomber disarming, I quickly analyze
An Engineer & also a linguist
I assess…& verbalize my feelings with a quickness
Just tryin to make a living, pay my bills
I'm a C-E-O, my purpose to fulfill
Why I'm here, on this planet
Don't have to get it booboo, it's not you who planted
This seed to…do this here

it's ﷲ that made…this path for me clear

[PAUSE]

I'm a lover, not a fighter
But I will throw down
Jersey girl but fighting learned in the Boogie Down
Won't allow you to come in
try & ruin
My spirit or my joyful nature
We can take it back to…Naughty By Nature
Or actually Public Enemy
Shut em down but then you'll be mad at me
Cuz I wouldn't entertain you
Bitter cuz you couldn't…change my point of view
See, me, I'm quiet & nice
But my alter-ego, sharp, she cuts like a knife
More a machete really
Need to catch up? Listen to Her Story
Uncontrollable…once unleashed
Doing you a favor by containing that beast
We get that from our Momma, she's a warrior too
She will cut you down, she's a giant at 5'2"
Or is it 5'5, I better get that right
Calling Mom short, she will end your life
Being checked by this quiet Desi won't feel good
So let's all be easy, keep it good in the hood
Avoid all of that, keep it positive
Cuz my purpose here…is really to uplift

This unjust world don't understand the pain

Why history repeats again & again
Hitler before…thought…that was done
& now Orange, same propaganda spun
Pitting us against each other, me against you
Black on brown or black on black, don't get it confused
Systemic oppression won't go down easy
Gotta stick together so Martin's dream can be
A reality
2019
Black Lives Matter still a tweet
or a hashtag?
when country built on slaves' backs
& then all of us immigrants
yet this fool thinks walls…are money well spent

This life just temporary, all just a test
& once it's over, I pray for the best
That's Jannah VIP, highest level at 7
My only goal, highest level of heaven
For my fellow math nerds, we can geek out on that
Don't come at me, please stop the attacks
Trying to hurt me personally, endangering my safety
Cuz I was Oprah in dev & now Oprah money making

& إن شاء الله, He HAS a plan

& I guess that's even…for my man
Cuz haven't met one yet that can handle me

& الله has shown me, He's really all I need

But…um…do want a family
& unless

Page 95 of 121

it's conception that's immaculate, He'll bring that man to me
A King, not a dictator
Secure man knows, won't be a hater
Of my skills or my edumacation
Supportive even if that's not his station
Dad always said book smarts mean nothing without street smarts
That's why you'll engineer & drive the car
Cuz there's more to life than just degrees
But let's be clear, I do have 3

Proud of that, my Dad taught me my worth
& told me never stay …with a man if he hurts
You or causes more pain…than happiness
No relationship is easy but it shouldn't be all stress
Always compromise…but never settle
So grateful to my Dad, deserved a medal
For the type..of…man he was
Didn't get much in this life
But hope he does above
Pray to meet you Daddy in Jannah VIP
Know you up there chillin with Muhammad Ali
& asking million questions, like you do
Pray to be reunited with you soon

But til ﷲ decides it's my time

I'll be here, just slaying these rhymes

Still optimistic, still have hope
Faith & community is how we'll cope
Let's recap, my focus is only heaven
Laser focused to keep it moving to 7

Jannah Firdaus, Jannah VIP

My one & only goal, إن شاء الله my destiny

Keep me in your prayers, I'm #duagreedy
& dua for all of us out here needing
Help & protection, feeling all alone

الله keep me safe until You call me home

الله keep me safe until You call me home

الله keep me safe until You call me home

The Block to the
Boardroom

Know ﷲ Loves Me

Noura:

My entire life has
Led up to this moment
Every single blessing & every single torment
All of it, leading me to this
Taking a risk
to challenge this business

Tahujjud doesn't see me often
But when it does, it's really quite awesome
Clarity, on what to do
Who I should be, to stand in my truth
Had a lot of interests, liked a lot of things
Struggled to claim them, scared of people judging

Thought I had to choose, pick only one
Wasn't sure how, they're all so much fun
Then I heard Queen Issa, speak her truth
Stand in her power, knew what to do
So innovative, there was no blueprint
She's the blueprint now, out here doing it

Inspired me, to do the same
ﷲ made it clear, it's all in His name

ﷲ made it clear, it's all in His name

The Block to the
Boardroom

الله made it clear, it's all in His name

[HOOK]: Know الله Loves Me!

All the trials prepared me all along
To handle the hate, in my faith stay strong
Cuz of my childhood
Experiences he gave me
Flow in mad spaces, He's the one that made me

Quote Tupac, recite the Quran
Not Benita Applebaum, He's the one that put me on
His path, to live in his service
Every act in my life is a form of worship
Viral or not, He sees it all
His top 10 list, only one I want
His…only pleasure I seek
He won't let me hide
Or shy away weak
Wants me strong, so strong I will be
Call it arrogant but He sees me

Claiming my power, bothers you huh
Doesn't sit right, not what you want
Muslim, woman, melanated, bolder?
Don't really care boo, He made me a Warrior!

Standing here for Him, serving as His vessel
Only through Him, will I reach another level

Pushes me
to don my hero suit
My hijab, pure heart, His pleasure I pursue
Accept His challenge, to claim my destiny
Through him, Oprah I will be
Get down now, BF me like Gayle
Or get out of the way, cause He won't let me fail

No we cannot still be friends
Must mourn you as if you're dead
Anything else would kill me instead.

Don't hate you, the opposite
Love you too much for this
Facade that our end didn't rip

Apart my soul, my heart, my life
Overwhelming grief pierced worse than a knife
Yearning for death gave me new life

الله all I need, all I have, all I love

Unconditional, all-consuming love

Through Him, جنّة فردوس إن شاء الله

true love

Know الله Loves Me!

Q & A with Hendeca:

Q: Could you describe your journey to this point. What made you want to write this book?

A: Thank you for phrasing it that way. I've heard "You weren't a writer before or your background isn't in writing…." which is inaccurate. Most artists, whether that's writer, painter, etc. are artists regardless of whether they're getting paid for that work or whether we're allowing ourselves to explore that side. I've been writing short stories & poems since I learned to write. I was inspired to write this book I'm an avid reader & never see myself portrayed fully. Muslims, especially Muslim women, are shown as one-dimensional monolithic characters. Either we're the terrorist, oppressed, or completely abandoned our faith.

This couldn't be further from the Muslims, men & women, that I know personally. We're dynamic, flawed, & beautiful people & I wanted a story to reflect that.

Q: You refer to the collective experience of people with melanin (Black, Latinx, Indigenous, etc.) as melanated. What brought you to that term.

A: I thought a great deal about this. I never liked the term "people of color" because the term "colored" has such a negative connotation & colorism has wreaked havoc on every society. It's not just limited to the US. In India, where I'm from, women's skin is literally falling off because of bleaching creams they're using to try to lighten their skin.

It's interesting, in the black community, I'm considered "light-skinned" & in the desi community I've been called "darkie" so people's perceptions of skin are all relative.

I also reject the term "minority" & "marginalized community" because we're not a minority anymore & we're only marginalized because white privilege & oppression marginalized us.

I reject being viewed relative to a white person & wanted a term that more positively described our collective experience. To me, "melanated" evokes more pride & power. It resonates with me.

Q: What was important to you about writing it in this format, as a novel-in-verse?

A: I grew up listening to Hip-Hop & am impressed at its ability to express such important, painful, & profound topics in 16 bars & a hot beat. Original hip hop was giving voice to a community that wasn't represented anywhere else.

Songs like "Runnin", "Only God Can Judge Me", "Mind Playing Tricks One Me" (MPTOM), "Waterfall" all had powerful messages. MPTOM was referring to mental health in the black community when no one was talking about it. Barely anyone is still talking about it!

In addition to my parents & the masjid, the black community had a large hand in raising me. I grew up in a black & Latinx neighborhood. Not only was I invited to the cook-out, I was made to feel a part of the family.

Tupac's "Keep Ya Head Up" had a deep impact on me. As الله encourages me to embark on this exciting new endeavor, I pay homage to the black community & Hip Hop because of the its influence on me. Artists like Pac, Lauryn, KRS-One, Rakim, Tribe, LL, Nas, Jay, & too many others to name. All Pac's words were eloquent & powerful. These words particularly stayed with me since I first heard it in the nineties: "I guarantee I will spark the brain that will change the world."

It was profound & I thought "Maybe I too will spark the brain that changes the world إن شاء الله.

There's eloquent storytelling in hip-hop & I pay homage to that.

Also found it easier to write in verse. Every time I sat down to write "a novel", it would quickly overwhelm me. Whereas writing lyrics comes naturally to me. A beat forces clean & concise language. No matter what you want to say, if it's off-beat, it won't work!

Lengthwise as well, there's a reason that songs aren't 20 minutes long. A song, or verses, mandate that you get to the point quickly & I love that. It made my writing stronger.

Q: That's a lot of Tupac. Clearly, you're a Tupac fan though you grew up in the East Coast. How'd that happen? There was such a tense rivalry between East & West when you were growing up. Some believe that's what led to both Tupac & Biggie's deaths. What made you "jump sides" so to speak.

A: I have a quick funny story about that. My Mom, a traditional India woman, comes home one day & is visibly upset. I ask her what's wrong & she says "Did you hear. Biggie got killed!". You have to imagine that with a thick Desi accent. It made me laugh because my Mom is not a hip-hop head at all & I had no idea she even knew who Biggie was. But that's my Mom, she surprises you with what she knows mashﷲ.

Also, I disagree that the rivalry is what killed them. Systemic oppression & white supremacy culture led to their deaths. Tupac always loved New York. He said himself that he had no beef with NY, it was against Biggie. & that was because he thought Biggie set him up to get shot. Regardless of whether that was true or not, this is what he believed at the time.
Again, this circles back to mental health. Tupac felt attacked & didn't know who he can trust. I've been there, thankfully never shot Alhamdulillah, but I'm a survivor of multiple traumas (9/11, molestation, sexual assaults).

Unless you get the proper care & make self-care a priority, the Shaitan will needle his way into your thoughts. Shaitan will make you believe no one cares & that ﷲ has forsaken you.

I believe that's what happened to Pac. He was a genius ahead of his time. Listen to any of his songs or interviews now & they're still relevant. He made some very poor choices because he lost sight of the fact that الله made him.

Tupac's story to me is both inspirational & a cautionary tale on what could happen if you forget the Creator Astaghfurla.

Q: That's a great segue into wellness & mental health. You've said you want to remove all gaps. Could you expand on that more?

A: Absolutely. In addition to, or because of, the wealth & education gaps, there is a wellness gap in this country. The ones that have access to wellness (mindfulness, yoga, etc.) are usually rich white people. It's rare for a melanated person to have the time, luxury, & resources to access wellness.

Numerous times I've been told, from melanated communities, "Wellness (or yoga or therapy) is for white people!" We've been taught to believe this as if we're not good enough for it or asking for help is a sign of weakness. This is how systemic oppression works by making us feel it's out of our reach & why bother.

Additionally, during my training for my yoga certification, I was confronted with so much white privilege! It surprised me to be honest. I'd practiced yoga for years & never noticed it. The difference once you become a teacher is that the insecure white people, those with white fragility, immediately feel threatened by you. They think you're trying to test them or, again because of their own insecurity, they feel inauthentic.

A white male yoga teacher verbally assaulted me and accused me of "losing the essence of yoga." Irritated me initially #whitePrivilege much? I "K-dubbed" myself, i.e. examined what I was feeling & why. Realized this was his attempt to invalidate me and/or project his ish onto me.

Once I identified that, refused to give it any power. Know I'm centered when I can laugh in situations like this & I did.

Even asked him "You don't see the irony in you, a white man all Lululemon-ed out, telling Desi woman that she's changing yoga too much?" & he didn't. He was too much in his feelings.

Q: Do you consider yourself a feminist?

A: Absolutely! Islam was the first religion to give women property rights in inheritance. Khadijah (ra) was the Prophet's employer before she proposed to him. She was the Oprah of her day & a feminist before that was even a word!

She was also a warrior ما شاء الله. I love the story of her climbing the mountain to Hira to bring food to the Prophet (ﷺ). That climb was no joke! People are barely able to do it now & she did it then, in the dark, with the threat of attack. That's why she was given سلام, سبحان الله! That's a warrior ما شاء الله & she's my example of the type of businesswoman, wife, & mother I hope to be إن شاء الله

The Block to the
Boardroom

Suggested Discussion Questions for Book Club

1. What were your initial thoughts after the first chapter regarding the trial?

2. Based on your answer to question one, what preconceived notions does this reveal that you held for the characters?

3. What drove Noura to take the action she did?

4. Which character resonated the most with you & why?

5. Were you surprised by the outcome to the trial?

6. Did white fragility &/or white privilege play a role in Noura's experiences?

7. How has white privilege &/or white fragility played out in your life, if at all?

8. How did Noura's friendships with Khadijah, Isabella, & Sara factor into the trial?

9. Why was it important that a loving black relationship were highlighted?

10. Were you satisfied with the ending? If so, why? If not, what would you have liked to be different?

11. What, if any, conversations has this sparked for you to have in your own life?

The Block to the
Boardroom

Recommended Resources

Though not a Muslim Wikipedia & prefer people do their own research, do recognize there are confusing & conflicting websites on Islam. Therefore, providing these resources since I personally trust them as reputable & credible. This is not an exhaustive list & cannot represent all ~2 billion Muslims because not one resource could. This is a starting point to learn more about Islam/Muslim practices in the US &/or if you're hoping to engage in Muslim spaces:

Yaqeen Institute: https://yaqeeninstitute.org

Qalam Institute: https://www.qalam.institute/

Khalil Center: https://portal.khalilcenter.com

CAIR:
https://www.cair.com/guide_to_challenging_islamophobia

The Block to the
Boardroom

Suggested Reading:

	Source	Notes
Quran		Translations vary. Scholars provide recommendations. Personally, I trust guidance given by:
Sunnah		♥ Sheikha Iesha Prime
Hadith	Bukhari	♥ Sheikh Omar Suleiman
		♥ Sheikh Yasir Qadhi
		♥ Sheikh Abdul Nasir Jangda
		♥ Ustadh A. Rahman Murphy

title	author
Freedom is a constant struggle	Davis
Palestine: Peace not apartheid	Carter
White Fragility	D'Angelo
Microaggressions	Sue
Power of Habit	Duhigg
Zig Zag	Sawyer
Emotional Agility	David
Calling in the One	Thomas

The Block to the
Boardroom

Acknowledgements

Thank you الله for always protecting, guiding, and loving me. I pray to realize Your purpose for me in this life & to have the courage, resiliency, & support, to live out that purpose. Pray to stay mindful that Yours is the only pleasure I should seek, Yours is the only protection I need, You are the only true source of health, wealth, & contentment. Ameen.

I love you, جزاك الله خير & thank you to:

Mom & Dad: Eternally grateful to you. Impossible to repay you for your humility in starting over, the hard work, love, & protection. Please know it is appreciated. Immeasurably blessed & grateful الله chose you to be my parents الحمد لله. Pray we are reunited in جنّة فردوس.

RJ & Double T: Original squad/ride-or-die/Queen OGs ما شاء الله :

Looked out for this nerdy quiet girl struggling to find her place when you had no reason to do so. Protected me from haters and my own self-sabotage. Without you, who knows where I would've ended. I do know it would've been a completely different trajectory. Grateful الله sent you to protect me and be examples of real women & friends.

Abdel & Housseinatou: One of the many examples of Black Love and partial inspiration for Brown Sugar. It's great to see a melanated couple so in love & supportive of one another ما شاء الله. Abdel – thank you for believing in me & helping me when no one else did. You are a beautiful example of what it means to love for another what you love for yourself. جزاك اللهُ خير & thank you for being my COO/brother/BFF/confidante ما شاء الله. Pray الله rewards you with the best in this life & الآخرة.

The Block to the
Boardroom

Farah: You are the a beautiful example of someone that gives completely: time, money, love ما شاء الله. Since our Qasid days, you've remained in my heart and close to me though we may be physically far. You gave me "loads"! I appreciate our friendship, honest counsel, & laugh-crying through our most difficult times together. Look forward to whatever the future holds for both of our journeys إن شاء الله.

Fatimah: You are as close to me as a sister ما شاء الله. Since our meeting at that walk for hunger, you have fed my spirit & soul. I appreciate our friendship, honest counsel, & laugh-crying through our most difficult times together. Look forward to whatever the future holds for both of our journeys إن شاء الله.

Muzlefa: Even though we do not see each other often, الله always brings us together at the most perfect time الحمد لله. My beautiful, smart, sweet Hajji & Jordan BFF. You are the modern examples of the Muslims that gave every & anything to their Ummah.

Oyah: My BU BFF! Outside of my degree, you are my greatest gift from BU. Showed me the true meaning of sisterhood & generosity by inviting me to your home Christmas break our Freshman year. Always have & will always continue to be in awe of your spirit, beauty, & talents ما شاء الله

Jus/Dale/Ty: Rocking since undergrad & will continue until our 80s إن

شــاء الله! Thank you for being the first men in my life without ulterior motives. Real recognize real. Your hearts are pure & you've always moved with integrity ما شــاء الله. PS: Yoga! Don't make me visit any of you after hip replacement surgery…I *will* because I'm ride-or-die but you will hear "told you so!". We don't want that now do we?? (Did I just jinx myself into surgery?? Audu billah! Never إن شاء الله !)

To my amazing teachers that never get enough credit yet are so pivotal in children's lives: Mrs. Cardine, Mr. Vincentz, Mr. Daley, Ms. Maccagno, Mr. Davignon, Professor Noonan, Professor Ray, & Mr. Weinstein.

Even though Mr. Weinstein was our social studies teacher, he was the first person to see potential in me and my writing. He encouraged me and supported me when very few others did.

There are many others that have helped me. Though I did not list everyone here, I truly appreciate you. Thank you all for your love whether it was through a kind word, encouraging thought, or a smile, I love & appreciate you all الحمد لله!

The Block to the
Boardroom

99 Names of الله

	Attribute (Arabic)	Transliteration	Attribute (English)
1	الرَّحْمَنُ	Ar-Rahmaan	The Most Beneficent
2	الرَّحِيمُ	Ar-Raheem	The Most Merciful
3	الْمَلِكُ	Al-Malik	The Sovereign
4	الْقُدُّوسُ	Al-Quddus	from All Blemishes/ Most Sacred
5	السَّلَامُ	As-Salam	The Giver of Peace/ Free From All Blemishes
6	الْمُؤْمِنُ	Al-Mu'min	The Guardian of Faith
7	الْمُهَيْمِنُ	Al-Muhaymin	The Protector
8	الْعَزِيزُ	Al-Aziz	The Almighty
9	الْجَبَّارُ	Al-Jabbar	he Overpowering Lord
10	الْمُتَكَبِّرُ	Al-Mutakabbir	The Self-Gratifying
11	الْخَالِقُ	Al-Khaaliq	The Creator
12	الْبَارِئُ	Al-Baari	The Evolver
13	الْمُصَوِّرُ	Al-Musawwir	The Fashioner
14	الْغَفَّارُ	Al-Ghaffaar	The Most Forgiving

The Block to the
Boardroom

15	الْقَهَّارُ	Al-Qahhaar	One Who Has Control Over All Things
16	الْوَهَّابُ	Al-Wahhab	The Giver of All Things
17	الرَّزَّاقُ	Ar-Razzaq	The Sustainer & Provider
18	الْفَتَّاحُ	Al-Fattah	Remover of Difficulties/ The Maker of Decisions
19	اَلْعَلِيْمُ	Al-Alim	The All-Knowing
20	الْقَابِضُ	Al-Qaabid	The Constrictor
21	الْبَاسِطُ	Al-Baasit	The Extender of Provisions
22	الْخَافِضُ	Al-Khaafid	One Who Humbles or Abases
23	الرَّافِعُ	Ar-Rafi	The Exalter
24	الْمُعِزُّ	Al-Mu'izz	The Giver of Honor
25	الْمُذِلُّ	Al-Muzil	The Giver of Disgrace
26	السَّمِيعُ	As-Sami'	The All-Hearing
27	الْبَصِيرُ	Al-Baseer	The All-Seeing
28	الْحَكَمُ	Al-Hakam	The Maker of Immutable Judgements
29	الْعَدْلُ	Al-Adl	The Just

The Block to the Boardroom

30	اللَّطِيفُ	Al-Lateef	The Knower of Innermost Secrets/ The Benevolent
31	الْخَبِيرُ	Al-Khabeer	The Totally Aware
32	الْحَلِيمُ	Al-Haleem	The Clement
33	الْعَظِيمُ	Al-Azeem	The Magnificent
34	الْغَفُورُ	Al-Ghafoor	The All-Forgiving
35	الشَّكُورُ	Ash-Shakoor	The Grateful/ One Who Accepts Gratitude
36	الْعَلِيُّ	Al-Aliyy	The High
37	الْكَبِيرُ	Al-Kabeer	The Great
38	الْحَفِيظُ	Al-Hafiz	The Protector
39	الْمُقِيت	Al-Muqeet	The Controller of All Things
40	الْحَسِيبُ	Al-Haseeb	The Reckoner/ The One Who Suffices for Everything
41	الْجَلِيلُ	Al-Jaleel	The Majestic
42	الْكَرِيمُ	Al-Kareem	The Benevolent
43	الرَّقِيبُ	Ar-Raqeeb	The Watchful
44	الْمُجِيبُ	Al-Mujeeb	The One Who Responds to Supplication

The Block to the Boardroom

45	الْوَاسِعُ	Al-Waasi'	The Ample Giving
46	الْحَكِيمُ	Al-Hakeem	The Wise
47	الْوَدُودُ	Al-Wadud	The Most Loving
48	الْمَجِيدُ	Al-Majeed	The Most Venerable
49	الْبَاعِثُ	Al-Ba'ith	he One Who Resurrects
50	الشَّهِيدُ	Ash-Shaheed	The Omnipresent
51	الْحَقُّ	Al-Haqq	The True
52	الْوَكِيلُ	Al-Wakeel	The Guardian
53	الْقَوِيُّ	Al-Qawwiyy	The Powerful
54	الْمَتِينُ	Al-Mateen	The Firm
55	الْوَلِيُّ	Al-Waliyy	The Patron
56	الْحَمِيدُ	Al-Hameed	The Praiseworthy
57	الْمُحْصِي	Al-Muhsee	The One Who Records
58	الْمُبْدِئُ	Al-Mubdi	The Originator
59	الْمُعِيدُ	Al-Mueed	e Restorer/The Recreator
60	الْمُحْيِي	Al-Muhyi	The Giver of Life

The Block to the
Boardroom

61	اَلْمُمِيتُ	Al-Mumeet	The Giver of Death
62	الْحَيُّ	Al-Hayy	The Ever Living
63	الْقَيُّومُ	Al-Qayyoom	The Self-Subsistent
64	الْوَاجِدُ	Al-Waajid	The Inventor
65	الْمَاجِدُ	Al-Maajid	e One With Excellence & Veneration
66	الْوَاحِدُ	Al-Waahid	The One Unequalled
67	اَلاَحَدُ	Al-Ahad	The Only
68	الصَّمَدُ	As-Samad	ıe One Free From Want
69	الْقَادِرُ	Al-Qaadir	'he One with Authority
70	الْمُقْتَدِرُ	Al-Muqtadir	e One with Full Authority
71	الْمُقَدِّمُ	Al-Muqaddim	The Promoter
72	الْمُؤَخِّرُ	Al-Mu'akhkhir	The Postponer
73	الأَوَّلُ	Al-Awwal	The First
74	الآخِرُ	Al-Akhir	The Last
75	الظَّاهِرُ	Az-Zaahir	The Manifest
76	الْبَاطِنُ	Al-Baatin	The Hidden

The Block to the
Boardroom

77	الْوَالِي	Al-Waali	One who Exercises Power over All
78	الْمُتَعَالِي	Al-Muta'ali	One Far Above Creation
79	الْبَرُّ	Al-Barr	The One Who Treats with Kindness
80	التَّوَّابُ	At-Tawwaab	The Ever Relenting
81	الْمُنْتَقِمُ	Al-Muntaqim	The Avenger
82	الْعَفُوُّ	Al-Afuww	The Pardoner
83	الرَّؤُوفُ	Ar-Ra'oof	The Affectionate
84	مَالِكُ الْمُلْكِ	Maalik-ul-Mulk	Possessor of Sovereignty
85	ذُوالْجَلَالِ وَالإِكْرَامِ	alaali-wal-Ikram	The Lord of Majesty & Benevolence
86	الْمُقْسِطُ	Al-Muqsit	The Just
87	الْجَامِعُ	Al-Jaami'	The Assembler
88	الْغَنِيُّ	Al-Ghaniyy	The Free From Want
89	الْمُغْنِي	Al-Mughni	The Enricher
90	اَلْمَانِعُ	Al-Maani'	The One Who Prohibits
91	الضَّارَّ	Ad-Daarr	One Who Brings Distress
92	النَّافِعُ	An-Naafi'	The Benefactor

The Block to the Boardroom

93	النُّورُ	An-Noor	The Light
94	اهَادِي	Al-Haadi	The Guide
95	الْبَدِيعُ	Al-Badi'	The Deviser
96	اَلْبَاقِي	Al-Baaqi	The Eternal
97	الْوَارِثُ	Al-Waaris	The Supporter/ The Inheritor
98	الرَّشِيدُ	Ar-Rasheed	One Who Loves Virtue or uidance Towards Virtue
99	الصَّبُورُ	As-Saboor	The Most Forbearing

The Block to the
Boardroom

Transliteration (in order of appearance):

Bismillah Il-Rahman Il-Raheem	بسم الله الرحمن الرحيم
Alhamdulillah	ال حمد لله
inshAllah	إن شاء لله
mashAllah	ما شاء لله
Jazak Allah Khayr	جزاك لله خير
dua	دعاء
Allah humma kama has anta khalqi fahasin khulqi	اَهُمَّ كما حَسَّنْتَ خَلَقِى فَحَسِّنْ خُلُقِى
Jannah Firdaus	جنُّة فردوس
Shaitan	
Al-Akhira	الآخرة
Ḥawqala	لا حول ولاقوة إلا بالله
lā ḥawla wa lā quwwata illā billāh	الحوقلة
Audhu billahi min ash-shaytaan-ir-rajeem	أعوذ بالله
	مِنَ ٱلشَّيطٰنِ ٱلرَّجِيمِ

Notes
[intentionally left blank for creativity to flourish]

The Block to the
Boardroom

The Block to the
Boardroom